GERMAN CUISINE, WINES & BEERS

A Brief Introduction

PATRICK PATRIDGE

Dr. Patrick Patridge

CONTENTS

GERMAN CUISINE

There is no better way for you to explore Germany and its regions than by eating German food and drinking German beers and wines.

Something special is available for every occasion and palate – from authentic locally-sourced fresh food to high-end Michelin-star cuisine.

Traditional German cooking varies in menus and style from one city and region to the next and is really great value for money.

Its diversity is a result of Germany's history, geology and colourful landscapes, each region having its own traditional food restaurants and homegrown recipes.

Background statistics open windows of gastronomic

taste, opportunity and excitement both for locals and for visitors alike:

- **13 wine regions**

- **1,350 breweries and 6,000 beers**

- **1,500 varieties of sausage**

- **300 types of bread**

- **500 great tasting mineral waters**

- **over 300 Michelin-starred restaurants**

Add to this an amazing variety and range of takeaways, bistros, restaurants and beer gardens - together with thousands of regional wine, food and beer festivals.

What more could you ask for?

You will most definitely be spoilt for choice!

TRADITIONAL CUISINE

Germans enjoy eating rich, hearty and wholesome meals. Pork, beef and veal are popular in traditional German cooking and seasoned in many ways.

Game or *Wild* is also eaten at certain times of the year, often as *Ragout* or *Gulasch*.

Schnitzels are thin, boneless cutlets of pork or veal coated in breadcrumbs, and are served in umpteen variations in most local restaurants.

Schnitzel with *Grüne Soße* or Green Sauce is a healthy and delicious option if and when available.

Frankfurter Grüne Soße consists of sour cream, oil, vinegar, mustard and seven fresh herbs - parsley, chives, chervil, cress, borage, sorrel and salad burnet.

Potatoes or *Kartoffeln* are a staple food throughout Germany and each region has its favourite ways of preparing them, whether boiled, fried, baked or roast.

Knödel or potato dumplings are served with many meals, especially in the north. In the south, *Spätzle* (soft egg noodles) and *pasta* are more common.

Fermented cabbage or *Sauerkraut* is probiotic-rich, full of vitamins and often served with *Wurst* (sausage) – of which there are some 1,500 regional varieties.

The most popular include *Bratwurst* - served with either *Senf* (mustard) or tomato ketchup; *Weisswurst* - a staple in Munich's *Viktualienmarkt* (open air food market); and *Currywurst* - a must if visiting Berlin.

Steaming *Eintopf* soups and wholesome stews are quite common and especially enjoyed after skiing, walking, sailing or cycling excursions.

Fish has also gained in popularity throughout Germany in recent times. *Forelle* (baked, fried or steamed trout) being the most common dish.

Bachsaibling (brook trout) is also a good alternative in Alpine regions.

Fischbrötchen (bread rolls) are a must if visiting the *Altonaer Fischmarkt* in Hamburg, the Baltic coastline, or North Sea resorts. They contain either fried white fish with *remoulade* sauce, smoked cod, or *hering filet* with cucumber.

*Schollenfil*let (plaice fillet), *Seeteufel* (monkfish) and *Dorade* (sea bream) are regular staples in most seaside restaurants, served up with either boiled or fried potatoes and fresh seasonal vegetables.

Locally produced cheeses, cereals and dairy products also play important roles in traditional German cuisine and recipes.

Throughout the country, desserts made with ice-cream, yoghurt, apples, cherries, strawberries, red forest fruits and plums are also very tempting.

Mouthwatering cakes such as *Apfelstrudel* and *Black Forest* chocolate cherry cake are served with afternoon coffee or tea, while beer, wine, apple wine (*Apfelwein in Hessen*), apple juice and / or mineral water accompany most dishes as a beverage.

Weinschorle, Apfelweinschorle and / or *Apfelsaftschorle* - white wine, apple wine or apple juice mixed with local mineral waters - are also popular and refreshing alternatives.

GOURMET CUISINE

With over 300 *Michelin*-starred restaurants, you are invited to experience the boundless imagination and creativity of Germany's world-famous chefs.

Explore Germany's award-winning kitchens and discover exceptional cooking alive to the joys of culinary delight and warm hospitality - from romantic Rhineland castles to downtown *Hamburg* hotels, and from Black Forest retreats to broad Baltic strands.

Savour gourmet dining and new interpretations of traditional cuisine. Relax and discern, eat with your eyes and enjoy exquisite meals filled with blissful aromas and heavenly flavours.

Nine three-star *Michelin* restaurants make Germany one of the most decorated fine-dining country in Europe; 46 restaurants currently have two stars, and another 272 have one.

297 restaurants have the *"Bib Gourmand"*, and 61 the *"Michelin Green Star"*.

One of the principal reasons for this award-winning success is the special emphasis placed on training and apprenticeship.

This guarantees consistent quality and perfect delivery of gourmet chefs' exceptional food ideas.

In German kitchens, the head-chef is very much part of a well-organized team, whose ultimate goal is the production of delightful dishes and excellent customer service.

Many *Michelin* restaurants serve a sophisticated blend of cuisine with original variations of regional classics and exciting new recipes - sometimes inspired by Germany's neighbouring countries, Switzerland and France, in particular.

Seasonal ingredients are highlighted and a 'lighter' side of German traditional cooking featured, including international crossover, vegetarian and vegan options.

Others present sophisticated French *nouvelle* and European cuisine with eye-catching artistic presentations.

DIETARY CONSIDERATIONS & CO2

"Seasoning does not just add flavour, it also enhances health. Herbs and spices are the only medicines which taste good."

Alfons Schubeck, *Celebrity German chef and cook book author*

Delicious food and beverages and great flavour are not only etched into our taste buds but are embedded in our sense of smell, and memories of travel. Inspiring culinary experiences are enjoyable topics of discussion and lively debate.

Diet is of increasing interest to consumers and travellers alike, as is the idea that you can do something beneficial for your health and the environment by choosing the right products, herbs, and spices.

The trend towards sustainability (*including food waste reduction*) plays an ever more important role in German food choices and German cuisine, with the health benefits of unprocessed, organic, and wholesome products having a priority.

Removing harmful food additives and reducing fat and sugar intake are also key considerations.

Fresh, seasonal, and local cuisine with creative presentation and friendly service in atmospheric settings is today in Germany a *sine qua non*.

In 2020, there were over 8 million vegetarians in Germany (*almost 10% of the population*) and some 1.6 million vegans (*2% of the population*).

The rapid growth of vegan products in Germany reflects a rise in ethical consumerism, especially among Millennials and Generation Z - or "*Fridays for Future*" - consumers.

Most Germans, however, are by no means giving up meat altogether, but are simply making room for more vegan and vegetarian options as part of what Alfons Schubeck has termed, a *"flexitarian"* and CO_2-friendly diet (Alfons Schubeck in 'Mal so, mal so - Meine Flexitarische Küche').

This culinary model presents ideas and opportunities for locally sourced (*shorter transport distances*), attractive, tasty, and plant-based food ingredients and beverage offerings.

A recent *Forsa* survey revealed that over 42 million people in Germany identify as *"flexitarians"* or *"part-time vegetarians."* It is estimated that over 20% of Germans eat mostly vegetarian.

Dietary requirements are no longer *niche* concerns but *creative culinary opportunities* that should neither be underestimated nor overlooked.

High-quality, healthy, and sustainable food with a low CO2 impact appears to be the way to go.

Scientists estimate that food production causes 35% of planet-warming, greenhouse gas emissions, with meat responsible for more than twice the pollution of fruits, grains, and greens.

In April 2022, an *Intergovernmental Panel on Climate Change* (IPCC) report urged world leaders, especially those in developed countries, to support a transition to sustainable, healthy, low-emissions diets to help mitigate the worst effects of the emerging climate crisis.

Eating less meat is one of the most meaningful changes people could apparently make to curb greenhouse gas emissions, help reduce deforestation, and even decrease the risk of pandemic-causing diseases passing from animals to humans, according to the IPCC report.

And the dietary shifts required to achieve this need not be extreme. Adopting a healthy *Mediterranean-style* diet – rich in olive oil, grains, vegetables, nuts, and moderate amounts of fish and poultry – could be nearly as effective as going full-on vegetarian or vegan.

If everyone met these basic nutritional recommendations, which for most people in developed countries means more fruit and veg and less red meat, CO_2 emissions could fall by 29% by 2050.

In Germany you will certainly be spoilt for choice!

GERMAN WINES

Germany is the 10th largest wine-producing country in the world. German wines are light, lively and fruity thanks to the climatic and geological conditions in Germany's thirteen wine growing regions.

Taste wines with the *Winzer* or wine growers, learn how the grapes are pressed, and celebrate new wines at seasonal *Weinfeste* or wine festivals.

And there are plenty of opportunities to do so because Germany has over 1,000 square kilometres of vineyards in its designated wine growing regions - the most northerly in the world.

German white wines are produced mainly from

Riesling and *Rivaner* grape varieties. White wine accounts for almost two-thirds of annual production.

Spätburgunder or *Pinot Noir* and *Dornfelder* are the most popular red wine varieties. Some of the red grapes are also used to produce *rosé*.

Total annual German wine production is around 8.5 million hectolitres (850 million litres), or ca. 1.2 billion bottles.

RIESLING

Germany is the home of *Riesling* wine with half of all *Rieslings* worldwide produced here. *Riesling* vines grow in all German wine regions and represent German wine culture like no other grape. In the *Rheingau* alone, *Riesling* grapes take up some 80% of the cultivated area.

Young light *Riesling* wines from crispy dry to fruity sweet are ideal Summer wines. *Riesling* is also a popular companion to freshly harvested asparagus in early Summer, served up with *sauce hollandaise* and new jacket potatoes.

Riesling grapes are also ideal for sparkling wine - or *'Sekt'* - production because of their natural acidity.

MÜLLER-THURGAU (RIVANER)

Müller-Thurgau is a crossing of *Riesling* with *Madeleine Royale* and a relatively new grape variety used to make flowery and lively white wines.

It is grown in nearly all of Germany's wine regions.

When you see *Rivaner* on the bottle label you can be assured that it is a light, fresh and dry wine.

SILVANER

Silvaner is used to produce dry, full-bodied fruity wines – particularly in Franconia or *Franken* where the limestone and *Keuper* soils ensure the production of very special wines.

Some 75% of German *Silvaner* vines are grown in Franconia and *Rheinhessen*.

Silvaner wine has mild acidity and is often blended with other varieties such as *Riesling* and turned into dessert wine.

GRAUBURGUNDER

Grauburgunder is a white wine grape with a grayish-blue fruit grown mainly in *Baden, Rheinhessen* and the Palatinate (*Pfalz*).

The grapes grow in small pine cone-shaped clusters.

Dry, spicy *Grauburgunder* wines vary in colour from light to deep golden yellows and amber.

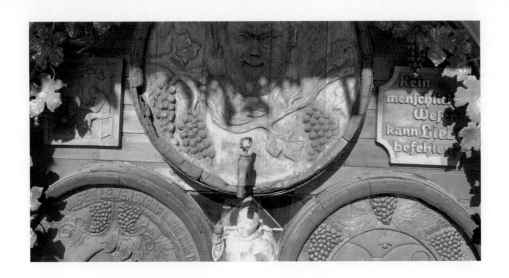

SPÄTBURGUNDER (PINOT NOIR)

Spätburgunder or *Pinot Noir* is the most popular German red wine grape variety.

It produces light to medium body wines, which come in a broad range of enticing bouquets, flavours and textures.

Spätburgunder is also a grape that requires complex viticulture skills on the part of the wine growers due to its high demands on climate and soils.

Some of the oldest and largest German red wine producers are to be found in the river *Ahr* valley in *Rheinland-Pfalz*. Its wines are marketed under the *Rhein-Mosel* label.

DORNFELDER

Dornfelder is an easy to grow, dark-skinned variety of red wine grape with good acidity.

It is the most successful newcomer of German origin (1955), now firmly established as the second-most grown red wine grape variety in Germany, in the Palatinate and in *Rheinhessen* in particular.

GERMAN WINE FESTIVALS

There is no better place to sample and enjoy German wines than in the landscapes and regions where they are produced and with the people who produce and sell them.

And there is certainly no better way of you getting to know wine growers and Germans in person than sitting down with them and rubbing shoulders at one of the thousand or so wine festivals over a glass or two of locally-produced wine or grape juice mixed with mineral water - and learning to speak some words of German - or even dialects of the same.

Most German wine festivals occur in the Summer and Autumn times of the year when the countryside is brimming with activity and full of natural colour.

They feature *Weinköniginnen* (Wine Queens), harvest parades, live music, dancing, fireworks and regional delicacies such as *Winzersuppe* (sausage & vegetable soup) and *Zwiebelkuchen* (onion cakes).

Particular favourites of mine are the annual *Rheingauer Weinmarkt an der Fressgasse* in downtown *Frankfurt am Main* and the *St. Albansfest* in *Bodenheim* (near *Mainz*).

And a final tip for German wine lovers: *Straußwirtschaften* - seasonally-opened wine restaurants in the Palatinate, *Rheinhessen* and *Rheingau* where wine growers sell and serve their own wine along with a variety of simple but delicious cheeses, breads, soups and *Wurst*.

You will know when a *Straußwirtschaft* is open by the vine branch, vine wreath and / or hand-made broom placed at outside the entrance.

So take some quality time out to explore the vine-covered slopes of the rivers *Mosel, Saar, Ruwer, Saale, Elbe, Nahe, Mittel-Rhein, Unstrut* and *Ahr*, and the gentle rolling vineyard hills of the *Pfalz, Hessische Bergstrasse, Franken, Baden* and *Württemberg* - by foot and by bicycle - or even by tractor-drawn trailer.

GERMAN BREWERIES

No other land on the planet has such a dense network of breweries including major global brand names and hundreds of small privately owned, family-run and monastic breweries with local brewing customs stretching back centuries.

And no other country has such an unbroken brewing tradition. This not only ensures the retention of the *Reinheitsgebot* (German Beer Purity Law) but also the maintenance of strong regional variety.

Diverse compositions of water, malt, hops and yeast are guarantors of a broad range of beers with different brewing and fermentation processes being applied.

GERMAN BEERS

Germany is often considered a Paradise on Earth for beer lovers. Germans are proud of some 6,000 beers brewed in over 1,350 breweries, half of these in Bavaria alone – in other words a different beer for every day for over 16 years!

Most German beers are brewed according to the *Reinheitsgebot* or beer purity law tradition from 1516, which only permits the use of water, malt, hops and yeast in the brewing process.

Some beer fans argue, however, that this has often led to stagnation regarding appearance and taste.

An important criticism, indeed, and one that is being

seriously addressed by many traditional breweries currently being challenged by a vibrant and growing *Craft Beer* movement.

Freshly poured German beers provide cool refreshment on hot Summer days and are best enjoyed with *Bretzeln* and grilled sausages in one of the country's many beer gardens.

The Munich *Oktoberfest* with its specially brewed *Festbier* is one of the largest public festivals in the world - with over six million visitors making the annual pilgrimage to the *Theresienwiese* with its large *Bierzelte* (beer tents) and non-stop live music.

Golden-brown, spit-roasted chicken (*Hendl*), roast pork knuckles (*Schweinshaxe*) and pork chops soaked in gravy (*Schweinsbraten*) are favourite beer tent dishes throughout Germany, along with *Kaiserschmarrn* (lightly-sweetened pancakes) and *Bayrische Creme* for dessert.

Beer has also found its way into German cuisine with renowned gourmet chefs seeking suitable beer combinations for their offerings, often including select beers in delicious culinary creations.

LAGER, EXPORT

Lager (a storeroom or warehouse) is a type of beer that is conditioned at low temperatures, normally at the brewery. It may be pale, golden, amber or dark in colour.

Although one of the most defining features of lager is its maturation in cold storage, it is also distinguished by the use of special yeast.

A pale *Lager* usually has fewer hops than an *Export* beer.

Export beer is a soft-textured pale lager beer influenced by the *Pilsener Lager*, which in former times could be exported beyond city limits. *Export* beers are traditionally brewed in *Dortmund*.

As the name suggests, *Export* beers were brewed for export to foreign countries and were brewed stronger in order to overcome long-distance transport. The increased original wort and alcohol levels ensured stability and durability.

WEIZEN OR WEISSBIER

Weizenbier and *Weissbier* are the standard German names for wheat beers characterized by a fruity-spicy flavour.

80% of *Weizen* beers originate in Bavaria but they are also very popular throughout Germany, especially in Summertime.

Weizenbier is available as filtered *Kristall* / crystal clear or as unfiltered *Hefeweizen* (yeast *Weizen*).

BOCK

Bock beers are strong heavy-bodied, bottom-fermented, bittersweet lagers darkened by high-coloured malts.

The tradition reaches back over 800 years to the Hanseatic city of *Einbeck* in Lower Saxony.

Maibock is a pale, strong lager brewed in the Springtime and frequently served at *Tanz in den Mai* and Maypole festivals.

PILSENER

Pilsener or simply *Pils* is a crispy refreshing pale lager beer with a light body and a more prominent hop character named after the Czech *Pilsner* bottom-fermented brewing process, invented by a Bavarian master brewer in the Czech town of *Pilsen*.

Pils is the most consumed type of beer in Germany and is available in many variations, also as *Export, Lager* and *Spezial*.

KÖLSCH

Kölsch is a pale, light-bodied, slightly bitter top-fermented beer which, when brewed in Germany, can only legally be brewed in Cologne where it has been brewed since the 12th century in the shadow of the city's magnificent Gothic Cathedral.

Kölsch is traditionally served in thin 0.2 litre glasses to help preserve its smooth taste and frothy foam. *Kölsch* beer halls in downtown Cologne are a must when visiting this ancient and highly sociable city situated on the banks of the majestic Rhine.

Kölsch is frequently enjoyed along with large portions of boiled ham and *Sauerkraut* - especially during *Fastnacht* or *Karneval in Köln*.

ALTBIER

Altbier is a top-fermented, lager beer brewed according to an 'old' tradition since the 13th century in *Düsseldorf* which made it possible to ferment and mature beer at higher temperatures.

In former times this was very important especially in the warm Summer months when stability and durability could not be guaranteed.

Altbier tastes range from mildly bitter and hoppy to very bitter and should be consumed in the Düsseldorf *Altstadt* or old city area - the *Längste Theke der Welt* - or the longest bar in the world, where over 250 bars, pubs and bistros are situated in close proximity.

BERLINER WEISSE

Berliner Weisse is a top-fermented beer brewed in a special *Berlin* manner.

It tastes bitter fresh and has low levels of alcohol.

Berliner Weisse is popular in Summertime and often served with a drop of either *Waldmeister* (woodruff) or raspberry syrup.

ALCOHOL-FREE BEERS

Alcohol-free or *Alkoholfrei* beers are on the rise in Germany are available in numerous variations from alcohol-free lager to alcohol-free *Weizen* beer.

They are isotonic, nutritious and very popular with cyclists, walkers, golfers and other sportspeople.

CRAFT BEERS

A craft brewery is a brewery that produces small amounts of beer, is typically much smaller in scale than the larger breweries, and is independently owned.

German craft breweries lay particular emphasis on quality, flavour and brewing techniques, with old recipes being resurrected, re-adapted and new beers being created.

Craft beers are increasingly popular and more widely available in Germany with innovative new breweries sprouting up all over the country.

Traditional breweries are also experimenting with their own craft beer creations. One of the first such breweries in Germany was established in Berlin in the mid-1990s.

New festivals and events such as the *Berlin Beer Week*, the *Braufest Berlin*, and the *Craft Beer Festivals* in *Frankfurt am Main* and in *Stuttgart* are testimony to growing consumer interest in diverse, nuanced beer creations and in a greater variety of beer types and flavours.

GERMAN BEER FESTIVALS

Germans like to celebrate in groups and there is no better place to get into the swing of things and to meet the locals than at one of Germany's many beer fairs and beer festivals.

The most famous of course being the Munich *Oktoberfest* (end-September to beginning October since 1810) which takes place under the motto of '*O ′ zapft is*'.

The *Oktoberfest* is the largest public fair in the world with some six million visitors and over five million *Maß Bier* drunk in large beer tents from traditional decorated 1-litre stoneware mugs called *Beer Steins*.

The classic *Oktoberfest* menu is a typical Bavarian *Schmankerl* consisting of *Weisswurst,* grilled half-chicken and Pretzeln. Munich brewers also brew a special festival beer known as *Festmärzen.*

Live music and dancing is non-stop and most participants wear traditional Bavarian costume, *Dirndl* for ladies and *Lederhosen* for gentlemen.

Oktoberfests have spread throughout Germany and further afield in recent times, complementing the many other regional and seasonal festivals such as the *Gäubodenfest* in *Straubing / Niederbayern* (August).

The *Cannstatter Folk Festival* in *Stuttgart* (end-September to beginning October) is another of the world's biggest festivals and a welcome haven for beer lovers.

This *Bierfest* serves not only *Stuttgarter* and *Swabian* beers but up to 100 German beers from the Baltic Sea to Upper Bavaria, and from the Rhineland to the *Oder* basin - a wonderful opportunity to sample, explore and get to know the breadth, depth and diversity of Germany's unique beer traditions and picturesque landscapes.

CULINARY CHRISTMAS

Many popular Christmas traditions originate in Germany – Christmas trees, *Erzgebirge* carved wooden figures, *Lauscha* glass Christmas tree balls, *Herrenhuter Sterne* (colourful stars), *Nußknacker* (nutcrackers), Advent wreaths and Advent calendars to mention but a few.

Thousands of *Weihnächtsmärkte* (Christmas Markets) with their historic traditions, carousels, Yuletide pageants, arts & crafts and culinary delights attract visitors from near and far, and food-lovers, too.

The most famous of these include Germany's oldest Christmas market, the *Striezelmarkt* in Dresden, the magnificent *Christkindlmarkt* in Nuremberg and the *Römerberg* in Frankfurt am Main.

Every village, town and city has its own special attraction or memorable Christmas highlight.

Kassel (in *Hessen*), for instance, has the largest fairy-tale pyramid and *Schlitz* (also in *Hessen*) the worlds largest Christmas candle.

Leipzig in Saxony has its magical *Thomaner Chor* and the enchanting choral music of *Johann Sebastian Bach*.

The German *Hauptstadt* or capital city, *Berlin*, has some sixty Christmas markets alone, the largest being in *Spandau* with a total of 250 stalls and stands.

Cologne, with its magnificent Gothic Cathedral, is a magnet for visitor groups from Belgium, the Netherlands, UK, Ireland, China and the United States.

And there are so many exciting things for visitors to see and do and so many fine delicacies to sample:

- Stroll through festively decorated, brightly lit, pulsating and seasonally scented squares, lanes and thoroughfares with wafting aromas of cinnamon, aniseed, cloves and muscat.

- Mingle with the locals while listening to the charming sounds of hand bells, carol singers and loden-clad trumpeters.

- Enjoy traditional delicacies such as *Gänsebraten mit Rotkohl & Kartoffelklöße* (roast goose with red cabbage and potato dumplings), *Kartoffelpuffer* (potato pancakes), *Bratwurst* (pork sausage), *Stollen* (fruit cake), *Lebkuchen* (gingerbread) or *Spekulatius* (seasoned spicy biscuits) - all washed down by a cup of steaming hot *Glühwein* (mulled-wine) or heartwarming *Feuerzangenbowle* (rum toddy).

- Followed by roast chestnuts & almonds, *Marzipan* treats from the city of *Lübeck*, *Frankfurter Bethmännchen* (marzipan & almond sweets) or assorted chocolate-coated fruits.

Frohe Weihnachten!

Merry Christmas!

GERMAN COOK BOOK TIP

"Deutschland - Das Kochbuch"

by Alfons Schubeck

(in German language only)

SOME CULINARY GERMAN

Guten Tag! - Hello!

Guten Abend! - Good evening!

Guten Appetit! - Bon appetit!

Zum Wohl! - Cheers! (wine)

Prosit / or Prost! - Cheers! (beer)

Rotwein - Red Wine

Weisswein - White Wine

Rosé - Rosé

Ein Glas Wein bitte! - A glass of wine please!

Ein Glas Sekt bitte! - A glass of sparkling wine please!

Ein Bier bitte! - A beer please!

Ein Schnitzel bitte! - A Schnitzel please!

Ein Steak bitte! - A steak please!

Bachforelle bitte! - River trout please!

Mit Salzkartoffeln? - With boiled potatoes?

Mit Bratkartoffeln? - With fried potatoes?

Mit Kartoffelpureé ? - With mashed potatoes?

Mit Reis? - With rice?

Mit Nudeln? - With pasta?

Mit Klöse? - With dumplings?

Mit frischem Salat? - With fresh salad?

Mit frischem Gemüse? - With fresh vegetables?

Probieren Sie! - Try this!

Vegetarisches Essen - Vegetarian Cuisine

Veganes Essen - Vegan Cuisine

Vielen Dank! - Thank you!

Dankeschön! - Thank you!

Bitteschön - You are welcome!

Wunderbar geschmeckt! - Tasted wonderful!

Sehr lecker! - Very Tasty!

Ausgezeichnet! - Excellent!

Bezahlen bitte! - I'd like to pay, please!

Auf Wiedersehen! - Goodbye!

Tschüß! - Cheerio!

DR. PATRICK PATRIDGE

FURTHER INFORMATION

German National Tourist Board

https://www.germany.travel/en/home.html

Deutscher Brauer Bund
(German Brewers Association)

https://brauer-bund.de/

Deutscher Weinbauverband e.V.
(German Winemakers & Vintners Associations)

https://www.dwv-online.de

Deutsches Weinbaumuseum in Oppenheim
(German Winemaking Museum)

https://www.dwm-content.de/

DEHOGA - German Hotels & Restaurants

https://www.dehoga-bundesverband.de/

Guide Michelin Deutschland

https://guide.michelin.com/de/de

Food and Drink, Beer and Wine Festivals

https://allexciting.com/food-drink-beer-wine-festivals-in-germany/

Berlin Beer Festival

https://www.berlin.de/en/events/archive/2852713-5437163-international-berlin-beer-festival.en.html

Cannstatter Volksfest Stuttgart

https://www.cannstatter-volksfest.de/en/landing-page/

Craft Beer Festival Frankfurt am Main

https://craft-festival.de/craft/

Craft Beer Festival Stuttgart

https://www.craftbeerfestival-stuttgart.de/

Oktoberfest Munich

https://www.oktoberfest.de/en

Bier- und Oktoberfest Museum München

https://www.bier-und-oktoberfestmuseum.de/#start

Gäubodenfest in Straubing

https://www.bayern.by/erlebnisse/stadt-land-kultur/feste/volksfeste/gaeubodenvolksfest-in-straubing/

Internationale Grüne Woche Berlin
(International Food & Drink Exhibition)

https://www.gruenewoche.de/

The Food & Beverage Industry in Germany

https://fmig-online.de/wp-content/uploads/2020/08/industry-overview-food-beverage-industry-en-data.pdf

Fresh Food & Vegetable Markets in Germany

https://www.wochenmarkt-deutschland.de/

GERMANY'S WINE REGIONS

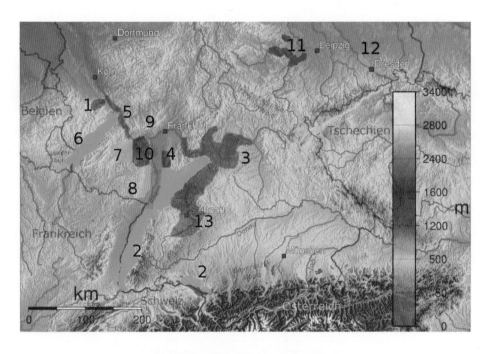

1: Ahr; 2: Baden; 3: Franconia;

4: Hessische Bergstraße; 5: Middle Rhine;

6: Mosel; 7: Nahe;

8: Palatinate; 9: Rheingau; 10: Rheinhessen;

11: Saale-Unstrut; 12: Saxony;

13: Württemberg

ZUM WOHL!

PROSIT!

THE AUTHOR

Dr. Patrick Patridge, born in Dublin, Ireland, has been living and working in Frankfurt am Main, Germany, since 1988, arriving there exactly one year to the day before the Fall of the Berlin Wall.

Patrick is a Tourism & Marketing Consultant, Historian, Geographer, Public Speaker, and a member of the German Castles Association - *Deutsche Burgenvereinigung e.V.*

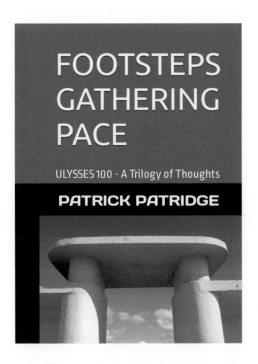

BOOK RECOMMENDATION

FOOTSTEPS GATHERING PACE
Poetry & Prose 1987 - 2022

"The vividly rendered details of memoryscapes and everyday life are extremely evocative ... FOOTSTEPS speaks to many people for so many idiosyncratic reasons."

Margaret Haverty
University of Tübingen

This is a compendium about the delights of spoken language and the magic of living words. A playful variety of poetry styles and contemporary prose.

Written in Dublin-English in Germany - with a tiny spattering of Gaelic and German in between! A *potpourri* of fantasy, fact and veritable fiction spanning six decades from Ireland to Germany.

For a quiet rainy day muse or to be read out aloud in the warm Summer sun!

Anecdotes and episodes recalling among many other themes:

Teenage Dublin Walkabouts, love and affection, a haunted Rhineland castle, Celtic Mythology, Guardian Angels, Bono's wedding reception, UCD Days, The Grove Social Club, Victorian Dublin, Count Dracula, the Good Friday Agreement, Gulf WarSpeak, Santa's New Grotto, the Eurovision Song Contest, *Salsa* dancing in Frankfurt, an Errant Medieval Knight and the vagaries of Life, the Universe and Everything.

Distilling thoughts, experiences and miscellaneous impressions gleaned over the years - both in Germany and in Ireland.

Characterised by light-hearted observations, philosophical meanderings, tongue-in-cheek banter and surreal metaphysical debate. Footsteps gathering pace, so to say, accompanied by quiet recollection, personal reminiscence and subtle reflection.

Includes **BERLIN WALL Recollections** and also **ULYSSES 100 - A Trilogy of Thoughts & Ten Poems** for the 100th anniversary year of the publication of James Joyce's ULYSSES in 1922 in Paris.

Review Prose

Like 'Ulysses', its puns and punditry, and its stream-of-consciousness perambulations compete and contrast abruptly with bold outbursts of straight prose and memoir of life before, during and after early schooling, university education and subsequent experience.

Covering decades of observation, with reference to history, culture, religion and mythology, including, at times, very cryptic allusion.

It might be read and/or spoken aloud like a self-contained, one-person show. Although its geography and tangents leap from Europe to Asia and even as far as the heavenly realm of angels and archangels, this is at heart an energetic discourse in latter day Dublinosity.

Review - Poetry

Well captured - the imagery of place and time and the complex weave of history, folklore, personal memoir and myth; obviously of Dublin and Germany and even ancient Gaul, but also of the deeper Irish layers of origin, from geology and topography through place names and tradition, up to the fleeting present.

There is the same Joycean allusion as in the prose, but not necessarily as Dublin-centric. It forces the reader to think of the value of time and place in the lives of everyone, passing through.

Patrick Long M.A.

Historian, Museum Curator & Contributor Dictionary of Irish Biography

Available to purchase from AMAZON stores online and worldwide in Kindle, Paperback (B/W photos), and Hardcover (colour photos).